T0417711

SHARK BIOLOGY

by Chelsea Xie

BrightP✦int Press

San Diego, CA

BrightPoint Press

© 2023 BrightPoint Press
an imprint of ReferencePoint Press, Inc.
Printed in the United States

For more information, contact:
BrightPoint Press
PO Box 27779
San Diego, CA 92198
www.BrightPointPress.com

LIBRARY OF CONGRESS CATALOGING-IN-PUBLICATION DATA

Names: Xie, Chelsea, author.
Title: Shark biology / by Chelsea Xie.
Description: San Diego, CA : BrightPoint Press, [2023] | Series: All about sharks | Includes
  bibliographical references and index. | Audience: Grades 10-12
Identifiers: LCCN 2022000359 (print) | LCCN 2022000360 (eBook) | ISBN 9781678203702
  (hardcover) | ISBN 9781678203719 (eBook)
Subjects: LCSH: Sharks--Juvenile literature. | Sharks--Physiology--Juvenile literature.
Classification: LCC QL638.9 .X54 2023 (print) | LCC QL638.9 (eBook) | DDC 597.3--dc23/
  eng/20220107
LC record available at https://lccn.loc.gov/2022000359
LC eBook record available at https://lccn.loc.gov/2022000360

CONTENTS

AT A GLANCE

- Most sharks have five types of fins. They have a dorsal, anal, and caudal fin. They also have two types of paired fins. These are pectoral and pelvic fins.

- Sharks have gills that allow them to take in oxygen from the water. Capillaries carry oxygen to the rest of the body.

- Shark skeletons are made of cartilage. This lightweight tissue is flexible, allowing sharks to make quick movements in the water.

- Sharks are cold-blooded. This means their body temperature is the same temperature as their surroundings.

- A shark's body shape, skin, and fins help the creature swim quickly.

- An oil-filled liver gives a shark energy to swim. It also helps the shark stay afloat.

- All shark reproduction begins with internal fertilization. After that, there are three different ways that sharks reproduce.

- Sharks have strong senses of sight, hearing, and smell. They can also sense electrical fields and changes in water pressure. All of these senses help sharks hunt.

INTRODUCTION

FEEDING FRENZY

An Atlantic blacktip shark whips its pointed tail from side to side. Its torpedo-shaped body pierces through the waters with ease. Water rushes over the shark's gills. The blacktip senses electrical pulses coming from a nearby school of fish. Their muscles create electrical pulses as they swim. The blacktip joins a group of other blacktip sharks. Together they herd the fish toward the shore.

The shark opens its mouth wide as it nears the fish. Sharp, knifelike teeth cut into

Blacktip sharks often hunt together in shallow waters.

The whale shark is known for its large size and gentle nature.

the fish. The blacktip shark has rows and

rows of teeth to replace any that get lost or

damaged. The scent of blood fills the water

as more of the sharks join the feast.

ABOUT SHARKS

There are more than 500 **species** of sharks. They swim in every ocean on Earth. Some sharks swim close to the surface. Others dive deep underwater. Sharks come in many colors and sizes. The whale shark is the largest type of shark. It can grow to be more than 33 feet (10 m) long. The dwarf lanternshark is less than 8 inches (20 cm) from head to tail. It is the smallest type of shark.

Even though there are many shark species, all sharks share common features.

They are fish. Like all fish, sharks have gills that allow them to breathe underwater. All sharks have skeletons made of cartilage. This is a type of hard **tissue**. Cartilage is found in the human nose and ears. The shape of shark teeth varies depending on diet. But all sharks have special teeth that help them eat their foods of choice.

Each part of a shark's body has an important function. Different body parts help sharks swim, hunt, and reproduce. These features make sharks some of the deadliest **predators** in the ocean.

A shark's gills are just one feature that allow it to survive in the ocean.

1

SHARK BASICS

A shark's biology helps it survive in the oceans. Biology includes body parts and their functions. There are several key body parts that all sharks share. They have gills. This allows them to breathe underwater. Gills are small slits near a shark's head. Most sharks have five gills.

The species with the most gills is the broadnose sevengill shark. As its name suggests, it has seven gills.

Inside the gills, there are small blood vessels called **capillaries**. When water

A sixgill shark has six gills. These gills help the shark get oxygen in the deep ocean.

Hammerhead sharks must keep swimming for water to pass over their gills.

flows over the gills, oxygen from the water passes into the capillaries. Capillaries and other blood vessels carry oxygen to the rest of the shark's body. Sharks need oxygen to survive. As oxygen enters the gills, carbon dioxide is released into the water.

This removes carbon dioxide from the shark's blood. Too much carbon dioxide causes health problems.

Frances Withrow is a **marine** scientist. She described how ocean animals breathe. "Marine animals also need oxygen to live," Withrow said. "It's just that they live off of dissolved oxygen, while we get oxygen from the air."[1]

Some sharks need to keep swimming to breathe. Water cannot pass over their gills if they stay still. For example, great white sharks must be in constant motion. They cannot get oxygen if they stop swimming.

Other sharks can breathe while staying still. The nurse shark sucks water in through its mouth. Then it pushes the water over its gills. This method allows the shark to stop on the ocean floor. But breathing this way takes more energy. Sharks use muscles

SPIRACLES

Some sharks have another body part called a spiracle that helps them breathe. A spiracle is a small slit behind each of the shark's eyes. Spiracles provide oxygen directly to the eye and brain. Sharks that spend most of their time deep underwater are more likely to have spiracles. This is because the deep ocean has less oxygen than the surface. Spiracles help these sharks take in additional oxygen.

in their mouths to suck in water. It is more tiring for sharks to pump water over their gills than it is for them to keep swimming.

Fins are another important part of a shark's biology. The size and shape of these fins differ between shark species. The fin on a shark's upper back is one of its most recognizable features. This fin is called a dorsal fin. Some sharks have a second dorsal fin on their lower back. In addition, most sharks have four other types of fins. This includes the anal fin, which is on the shark's belly. It is close to the tail.

SHARK PARTS

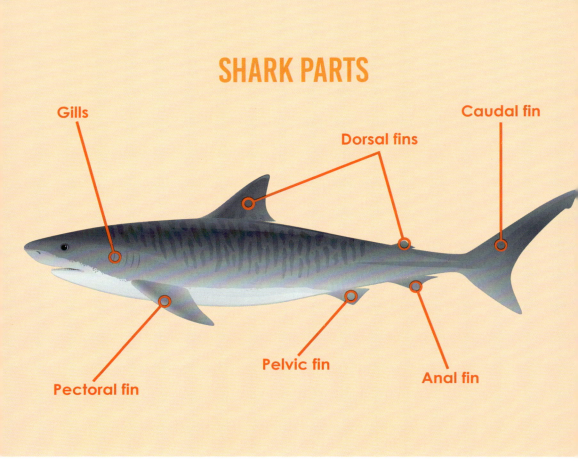

Gills

Dorsal fins

Caudal fin

Pectoral fin

Pelvic fin

Anal fin

Sharks have many special body parts. These parts help them swim through the water.

The caudal fin is at the end of the tail. It is

also called a tail fin.

Pectoral fins and pelvic fins are paired

fins. This means that the fins are located on

the left and right sides of a shark. The two pectoral fins are close to the head. They are larger than pelvic fins. The two pelvic fins are near the shark's rear.

UNDER THE SKIN

A cartilage skeleton is another key part of a shark's biology. Many other types of fish have bony skeletons. Bones are hard. They protect soft parts of a fish's body, including its brain. But bones are heavy. Shark skeletons are lightweight because they are made of cartilage. Being light allows sharks to swim quickly. It helps them stay afloat.

Even though cartilage is softer than bone, it still provides protection.

People have cartilage too. This type of tissue is found in the ears and nose. It is also located in joints. Cartilage is flexible. It allows the joints to move and bend.

It improves flexibility in sharks as well. They are able to make quick movements in the water.

SHARK BLOOD

Sharks are cold-blooded. This means that a shark's body temperature matches the surrounding water. For this reason, most sharks live in warm water. Sharks are also more common close to the ocean's surface. Water temperatures become colder as the ocean gets deeper.

Sharks struggle to survive if they get too cold. Their muscles may not work correctly

A great white shark is able to keep its blood warmer than its surroundings.

when their body temperature is too low. The cold can affect how well their eyes work.

Mark Royer is an ocean biologist. He studies hammerhead sharks. He tracked a group of hammerheads 2,625 feet (800 m) below the surface. Temperatures at this depth can reach 40 degrees Fahrenheit (4°C). Royer wondered how the sharks were able to survive the cold waters. "If a [hammerhead] shark gets too cold, it can't keep itself moving and breathe," he said.[2] He thinks that these sharks may hold their breath to stay warm. The sharks may close their gills. This way, heat from their blood is not lost to the cold water.

STAYING WARM

There are five known species of sharks that can stay warmer than their surroundings. The great white shark is one species. It uses warmth from its muscles. Muscles release heat as they are used. Blood vessels surround the muscles in a great white shark. They capture heat from the muscles. Then the blood carries heat throughout the body. This keeps the shark warm.

2

HOW DO SHARKS SWIM?

Sharks are fierce predators. Many rely on speed to hunt fish and other food. Their biology allows them to swim skillfully through the water.

A force called drag slows things moving through the water. This force pushes against the shark when it swims. The shape of a shark's body is an essential part of its speed. Most sharks have sleek bodies. This shape allows the sharks to slice through the water with little drag. The mako shark is the fastest shark species in the world. It can swim 60 miles per hour (96 kmh). Like other quick swimmers, the mako shark has a torpedo-shaped body.

A mako shark's streamlined body helps it swim at fast speeds.

Skin texture also reduces drag. Shark skin may look smooth, but it has the texture of sandpaper. The skin is covered in tiny scales called dermal denticles. The scales point backward. Water flows over the skin without slowing the shark down too much.

DO SHARKS SLEEP?

Sharks have periods of rest and activity. Some sharks swim even while resting. The spinal cord may control this motion while the brain rests. Jay Bradley works at the National Aquarium in Baltimore, Maryland. He talked about resting periods in sharks. "They don't go into an unconscious state," he said. "We still don't fully understand what they do during rest periods."

Quoted in Sarah Gibbens, "Video Shows How Sharks 'Sleep' in Large Groups," National Geographic, August 1, 2017. www.nationalgeographic.com.

FIN FUNCTIONS

Fins play an important role in swimming.
A shark swims by swinging its tail from side
to side. The swishing tail fin pushes against
the water. It provides thrust. This is the force
that propels the shark forward. A shark's
tail fin is divided into upper and lower lobes.
The amount of thrust varies depending on
the shape of the upper lobe. The short,
crescent-shaped tail of the mako shark
provides a lot of thrust.

Sharks have a muscle that stiffens their
tails. The stiff tail can push against the
water with increased force. It provides

extra thrust compared to other fish tails. It helps shark outswim their **prey**. Scientist Brooke Flammang used imaging technology to track how a shark's tail pushes water. "[It] provides a big advantage," Flammang said of the tail muscle. "It may be allowing the animal to produce almost continuous thrust."[3]

Other fins have different roles. The pectoral fins on either side of a shark help it to turn while swimming. These fins also provide lift. They work like airplane wings, guiding the shark as it swims up and down. The pelvic, dorsal, and anal fins give the shark stability. They help the shark make fine movements while it swims.

Sharks have muscles in their fins and throughout their bodies that they use to swim. They have two types of muscle. Red muscle is used for continuous motion. The color comes from a **protein** called myoglobin. This protein carries and stores oxygen. Red muscle needs oxygen to

SHARK FINNING

Shark fin soup is a popular dish in some countries. Fishers catch live sharks and cut off their fins. The sharks are then tossed back into the ocean. A shark cannot survive without its fins. Shark finning is illegal in US waters.

Great white sharks may leap out of the water when hunting prey.

function. White muscle is the other type.

Oxygen is not needed when using these

muscles. Instead, the energy comes from

sugars stored in the shark's body. White

muscle is used for short bursts of speed.

Powerful muscles allow some sharks

to swim at fast speeds and leap out of

the water. This is called breaching. Great white sharks are known to breach while hunting seals. These 2,000-pound (910-kg) predators can jump 10 feet (3 m) into the air.

STAYING AFLOAT

Other types of fish have a swim bladder. This organ is filled with air. It keeps fish from sinking. But sharks don't have swim bladders. They depend on other features to stay afloat. Lightweight cartilage is one **adaptation**. Sharks also have oil-filled livers. Oil floats in water. The oil also provides sharks with energy. The size of a shark's liver depends on the species. Sharks that travel in the open ocean have larger livers than those that stay in shallow waters.

Sand tiger sharks have another method to help them float. They sometimes come up to the surface and swallow air. The air in their stomachs allows them to float in place. They are the only shark species known to show this behavior.

Sharks cannot swim when they are flipped upside down. In fact, many of them fall into a trance-like state called tonic immobility. Their breathing slows and their

Sand tiger sharks often hunt for prey near the ocean floor.

muscles relax while they float on their backs. Scientists may flip over a shark while studying it. They aren't sure why sharks show this behavior. It may be related to mating. Or playing dead may turn away predators. Sharks are able to come out of tonic immobility on their own. They flip back over when released by the scientists.

3

HOW ARE SHARKS BORN?

Sharks reproduce, or have their young, in three different ways. All shark reproduction begins with internal fertilization. This is the process of male sperm entering eggs inside a female shark's body. Male sharks have two structures called claspers, one near each of its pelvic fins. One or both claspers are inserted into the female, depending on the shark species. Sperm is released from the claspers and eventually reaches the eggs.

A fertilized egg develops into an embryo. Nutrients help the embryo grow and develop. It takes an average of twelve months for an embryo to develop into a baby shark. Shark babies are called pups.

A lemon shark pup swims near its mother.

Shark pups may hide under rocks and coral. This protects them from predators.

INTERNAL HATCHING

The first way sharks give birth is for fertilized eggs to hatch within the female shark. This is the most common process. It is called ovoviviparity. The eggs have yolk inside them. The yolk is full of nutrients for the developing embryo. After the pup hatches, it eats the remaining egg yolk. Pups typically hatch after three months. They continue to develop within the mother's womb. Pups are known to eat other eggs inside the mother. This gives them extra nutrients.

The mother protects the pup as it grows within her womb. This keeps the baby shark safe from predators. Pups stay in the womb between two months and twenty-four months. The time varies by species. Developing pups are not necessarily safe from each other. A sand tiger shark has two wombs. Only the largest pup survives

Sand tiger sharks can grow up to 10.5 feet (3.2 m) long.

in each womb. This is because sand tiger pups will eat other developing pups. Nature historian Sir David Attenborough talked about this act. "Inside each female, infant teeth are being put to good use, as the female's two largest unborn pups slowly eat their siblings," he said. "It ensures only the strongest and largest babies survive."[4]

LAYING EGGS

Some shark species release egg cases. These structures look different than bird eggs. Egg cases come in different shapes. Bullhead sharks lay egg cases that are shaped like spirals. But most egg cases are pouch-shaped with long tendrils. They are nicknamed mermaid purses. Other egg-laying sharks include catsharks and angel sharks.

Some shark pups develop inside egg cases.

This way of reproducing is called oviparity. Approximately 40 percent of sharks reproduce this way. The pup develops in the egg case outside its mother. Most egg cases hold one pup.

The tendrils on the egg cases curl around coral and seaweed. They keep the egg case from washing far out into the ocean. Egg cases are also covered in a sticky substance. This helps the egg case stay close to the shore.

The egg case has yolk that the developing pup absorbs for nutrients.

INDEPENDENT REPRODUCTION

In rare cases, zebra sharks have been able to reproduce without a mate. In 2017 Australian scientists documented female zebra sharks that laid egg cases in an aquarium. The egg cases had not been fertilized by a male shark. But pups hatched anyway.

The pup grows within the egg case. It usually hatches in six to nine months. Then the pup must find food for itself.

LIVE YOUNG

Some shark pups do not hatch from eggs or get nutrients from egg yolk. Instead, they receive nutrients from an organ called a placenta. The placenta connects the developing pup to its mother. Nutrients and oxygen flow through the placenta. It also removes waste from the pup.

This type of reproduction is called viviparity. It is also seen in other animals,

including humans. Hammerhead sharks give birth this way. They evolved relatively recently. The first shark existed 420 million years ago. In comparison, the first hammerhead is thought to have lived only 20 million years ago.

Reef sharks gather at Ningaloo Reef off the coast of Western Australia. Certain areas of the reef serve as nurseries for these sharks.

SHARK NURSERIES

No matter the type of reproduction, shark pups must fend for themselves after they hatch or are born. Female sharks may lay their eggs or give birth in shark nurseries. These are generally warm, shallow waters.

Shark nurseries include habitats such as coral reefs and seagrass beds. These locations provide cover from predators and often have plenty of food.

Female sharks return to the nurseries to reproduce. Some nurseries have existed for many years. In 2020 researchers identified an ancient great white shark nursery off the coast of Chile. They believe the nursery was used 5 million years ago. It is no longer used today. But the discovery gives scientists insight on shark behavior. The researchers wrote, "Our findings demonstrate that one of the top predators in today's oceans has used nursery areas for millions of years, highlighting their importance as essential habitats for shark survival."[5]

These studies are important because shark numbers are declining. Some sharks are killed for their fins. Others are accidentally caught in fishing nets. In addition, many shark species have long pregnancies. Many also produce only a few pups with each pregnancy. But sharks play an important role in the ocean. They improve ocean health. Sick and injured prey are easier to hunt. Sharks limit the amount

of sick and weak prey in the oceans.

Stefanie Brendl is the executive director of Shark Allies, an organization that works to protect sharks and rays. She talked about the importance of protecting sharks. "They keep our fish stock healthy," she said. "They keep the **food chain** intact, [and] they keep diseases out of other animal populations."[6]

4

HOW DO
SHARKS HUNT?

Sharks are apex predators. This means they are the top predators in their habitats. Adult sharks are rarely attacked by other animals. But they are skilled hunters. A shark's biology gives it many advantages while hunting for prey.

Sharks have specialized teeth that help them eat. Cookie-cutter sharks use their sawlike teeth to bite chunks out of large prey. Sharks that eat shellfish have flat teeth that help them break open shells. Whale sharks eat tiny creatures such as krill and plankton. These sharks have small teeth that aren't used while eating. Instead, they

Sharks may have many rows of teeth.

swallow mouthfuls of water. Pads in their

throats separate their prey from the water.

Most sharks have many rows of teeth.

They are able to replace teeth that are lost

or damaged. Some sharks can grow a

whole new set of teeth in just two weeks.

A shark may lose thousands of teeth

ADVENTUROUS EATERS

Some shark species have a preferred type of food. Tiger sharks are not picky eaters. They are nicknamed "the garbage cans of the sea." They eat fish, turtles, crabs, and many other animals. The sharks also eat dead animals. Because of the variety in their diets, pollution can be especially harmful to tiger sharks. Scientists have even found trash such as tires and bottles in the stomachs of tiger sharks.

throughout its life. Because it can regrow its sharp teeth, it is always prepared to hunt.

VISION

Strong senses give sharks many advantages while hunting. Vision is just one of the senses that allows sharks to be fearsome predators. Mikki McComb-Kobza is the executive director of Ocean First Institute. She talked about the important role of shark eyes. "The story of shark eyes is a story of tremendous diversity," she said. "To look into the eye of a shark is to really look back in time at all of the amazing adaptations that really benefit that shark in its current state."[7]

Sharks have eyes on the sides of their heads. This gives them a wide range of vision. They can see clearly at distances of up to 50 feet (15 m).

Light does not travel well underwater. The deep ocean can be very dark. Sharks that dive deep underwater have a special layer of cells at the back of their eyes. This is called the tapetum lucidum. Sharks that hunt at night also have this layer. The tapetum lucidum reflects light that enters the eye. It allows them to see clearly in

the dark. Some sharks may see ten times

better than humans in low light conditions.

HEARING AND SMELL

Sharks have a strong sense of hearing.

Their ears are located behind their eyes.

They look like holes lined with hair.

Sound waves strike the hairs and cause

them to vibrate. Sharks interpret these vibrations as sound. Some sharks are able to hear sounds made more than 1 mile (1.6 km) away.

A powerful sense of smell also helps sharks hunt. Using two nostrils on the underside of their snouts, sharks can detect scents that are hundreds of yards away. Their noses are especially sensitive

EYE PROTECTION

Some shark species have a thin covering that slides over their eyes. It protects their eyes when they hunt. The covering is like an eyelid. Great white sharks have another method. Their eyes roll backward in their heads as they lunge at prey.

to the scent of blood. They can detect a

teaspoon's worth of blood in an area the

size of a swimming pool. This lets them find

weak and injured prey.

OTHER SENSES

Sharks have two senses that humans

do not have. The first is electroreception.

This means that sharks can sense electric

pulses in the water. Muscles give off

faint electrical pulses. Organs called the

ampullae of Lorenzini detect these pulses.

These organs are located on a shark's head

and underside. Sharks can find their prey

even if they can't see, hear, or smell it. They sense the electrical pulses of a fish.

This sense may help sharks in other ways. Scientists think it allows sharks to travel long distances without getting lost. Magnetic fields surround the earth. Sharks can sense these fields with electroreception. They learn their position in the ocean.

The lateral line system is another sense that is important to sharks. Small pores create a line down the shark's body. These pores detect changes in water pressure. The movement of other creatures causes pressure changes. Pressure also changes

A shark's senses make it one of the most dangerous predators in the ocean.

when water crashes into objects. A sensitive lateral line system allows sharks to find prey and navigate the oceans. It also helps sharks sense water depth.

Sharks have many adaptations that help them survive. Biology gives sharks the powerful senses and strong muscles they need to be dangerous hunters.

GLOSSARY

adaptation

a part of an animal or a plant that allows it to survive well in its habitat

capillaries

small, thin blood vessels

food chain

a way to organize the animals and plants in an ecosystem based on which organism eats another

marine

of or relating to the seas and oceans

predators

animals that kill and eat other animals

prey

an animal that is killed and eaten by other animals

protein

a substance that helps the body function properly

species

a group of animals of the same kind

tissue

a group of cells that share a specific function

SOURCE NOTES

CHAPTER ONE: SHARK BASICS

1. Quoted in Tara Santora, "Can Fish and Other Marine Animals Drown?" *Live Science*, June 28, 2021. www.livescience.com.

2. Quoted in Liza Lester, "Shark May Avoid Cold Blood by Holding Its Breath on Deep Dives," *Phys Org*, February 20, 2020. https://phys.org.

CHAPTER TWO: HOW DO SHARKS SWIM?

3. Quoted in Elizabeth Pennisi, "How Sharks Go Fast," *Science*, November 29, 2011. www.science.org.

CHAPTER THREE: HOW ARE SHARKS BORN?

4. Quoted in Melissa Cristina Márquez, "Shark Cannibalism: It's a Thing and It Just Got Weirder," *Forbes*, December 29, 2018. www.forbes.com.

5. Quoted in Melissa Cristina Márquez, "First Evidence of Ancient Great White Shark Nursery," *Forbes*, May 18, 2021. www.forbes.com.

6. Quoted in Emma Brown, "A Coronavirus Vaccine Could Kill Half a Million Sharks, Conservationists Warn," *NPR*, October 10, 2020. www.npr.org.

CHAPTER FOUR: HOW DO SHARKS HUNT?

7. Quoted in Mark Price, "How Can You Tell a Great White Shark Is About to Attack? It's Their Eyes, Experts Say," *Miami Herald*, February 4, 2021. www.miamiherald.com.

FOR FURTHER RESEARCH

BOOKS

Madeline Nixon, *Great White Shark*. New York: AV2, 2019.

Ethan Pembroke, *The Shark Encyclopedia for Kids*. Minneapolis, MN: Abdo Publishing, 2021.

Brian Skerry, *The Ultimate Book of Sharks*. Washington, DC: National Geographic, 2018.

INTERNET SOURCES

Sarah Gibbens, "Video Shows How Sharks 'Sleep' in Large Groups," *National Geographic*, August 1, 2017. www.nationalgeographic.com.

Mark Price, "How Can You Tell a Great White Shark Is About to Attack? It's Their Eyes, Experts Say," *Miami Herald*, February 4, 2021. www.miamiherald.com.

"Shark Biology," Florida Museum. www.floridamuseum.ufl.edu.

WEBSITES

Ocean First Institute
www.oceanfirstinstitute.org

Ocean First Institute works toward ocean health through research and education. It is dedicated to getting youth involved in its efforts to protect the ocean and its creatures.

Shark Allies
https://sharkallies.org

Shark Allies focuses on making changes to protect shark and ray species worldwide. It raises awareness on issues such as shark finning and ocean pollution.

Shark Trust
www.sharktrust.org

The Shark Trust is an organization dedicated to the global protection of sharks. It encourages laws and practices that will keep shark populations safe.

INDEX

IMAGE CREDITS

ABOUT THE AUTHOR

Chelsea Xie lives in San Diego, California. She enjoys reading books on the beach, far away from sharks.